YOUR KNOWLEDGE HAS VALUE

Bibliographic information published by the German National Library:

The German National Library lists this publication in the National Bibliography; detailed bibliographic data are available on the Internet at http://dnb.dnb.de .

Imprint:

Copyright © 2017 GRIN Verlag
Print and binding: Books on Demand GmbH, Norderstedt Germany
ISBN: 9783346154552

This book at GRIN:

https://www.grin.com/document/536592

Florian Beyer

Fine trading and factoring. Methods of company funding

GRIN Verlag

GRIN - Your knowledge has value

Since its foundation in 1998, GRIN has specialized in publishing academic texts by students, college teachers and other academics as e-book and printed book. The website www.grin.com is an ideal platform for presenting term papers, final papers, scientific essays, dissertations and specialist books.

Visit us on the internet:

http://www.grin.com/

http://www.facebook.com/grincom

http://www.twitter.com/grin_com

Finetrading

Study Programme

Master of Business Administration (MBA)

Module:	International Investment & Controlling
Author:	Florian Beyer
Place, Date:	Hamburg, August 31, 2017

Table of contents

List of figures

List of abbreviations

SME   Small and medium-sized enterprises

1 Introduction

Ten years ago, from 2007 to 2011 the global financial and the euro crisis have caused a peak in bankruptcies of many companies and even states have experienced financial difficulties. Since 2011, the total number of companies' bankruptcies declines. In 2016, there were 21,518 insolvencies of companies in Germany. In contrast to this, in 2010, at the peak of the crisis there were 32,687 insolvencies.[1] Overall, most of the companies in Germany are small and medium-sized enterprises (SME). In 2014, they represented 99.3 percent of all companies in Germany.[2]

A proper working capital management is essential for all companies. Especially, SME are otherwise threatened to lack of liquidity or risk to become insolvent.[3]

Company funding has experienced profound changes lately. Basel I-III have extensively changed the regulatory circumstances for banks and their granting of credits. Banks have to comply with changed regulatory capital and liquidity requirements as well as with new debt caps. This has a strong influence on company funding. Therefore, the rating of a firm and the risk of an investment will increase the price of the company funding.[4] The changed importance of working capital management and the new regulatory requirements have altered companies' financing possibilities and partners. Moreover, the financial crisis has revealed their dependency on certain bankrollers.[5]

Thus, other methods of financing suchlike factoring, finetrading, leasing and crowdfunding increased their importance. This paper examines finetrading and factoring with regard to their differences, advantages, disadvantages and the methods' influence on the balance sheet.

---

[1] Statistisches Bundesamt, "Insolvenzen," https://www.destatis.de/DE/ZahlenFakten/Indikatoren/LangeReihen/Insolvenzen/lrins01.html;jsessionid=94B634D2EF272178D6D8092018C2007B.cae2, accessed August 2017.

[2] Statistisches Bundesamt, "Anteile kleiner und mittlerer Unternehmen an ausgewählten Merkmalen 2014," https://www.destatis.de/DE/ZahlenFakten/GesamtwirtschaftUmwelt/UnternehmenHandwerk/KleineMittlereUnternehmenMittelstand/Tabellen/Insgesamt.html, accessed August 2017.

[3] Eckstein, A., Liebetrau, A., and A. Funk-Münchmeyer, *Insurance & Innovation 2017 – Ideen und Erfolgskonzepte von Experten aus der Praxis* (Karlsruhe: Verlag Versicherungswirtschaft GmbH, 2017), p. 91.

[4] EY, "Wege zum Wachstum – Finanzierungsverhalten im deutschen Mittelstand," September 2013, http://www.ey.com/Publication/vwLUAssets/EY_Agenda_Mittelstand_-_Wege_zum_Wachstum_2013/%24FILE/EY-Studie-Wege-zum-Wachstum.pdf, accessed August 2017, pp. 9-11.

[5] Krings, Thomas, "Die Bedeutung der Lieferantenfinanzierung in der Unternehmenskrise," in *Refinanzieren statt Sanieren? – Unternehmen und Statten in der Krise,* edited by Werner F. Ebke, Christopher Seagon, Michael Blatz (Baden-Baden: Nomos Verlagsgesellschaft, 2014), p. 81.

First, a brief introduction of the Basel requirements is outlined. Second, finetrading, factoring and reverse factoring are defined and distinguished. Third, the advantages and disadvantages are explained. Finally, the influences on the balance sheet of the involved parties and on working capital are investigated.

2 Reasons for new company funding methods

There are two main drivers for a change and uprising of novel company funding methods. On the one hand, the numerous financial crises have established a new scope of requirements for banks represented in the Basel I, II and III regulations. On the other hand, working capital management and its optimisation have tremendously gained importance.[6] Thus, company financing is top-ranking but the traditional bankroller, the house bank, is no longer the sole partner for companies.

2.1 Implications of the Basel accords

In 1974, the Basel Committee on Banking Supervision was founded. It suggests requirements for the financial sector to unify supervisory rules. The suggestions have no legal force and represent a global, voluntary framework. Nevertheless, G20 and additional states transpose them into law.[7]

In general, the Basel accords are created to establish capital requirements for banks. Banks are granting credits but have to obtain their solvency. In short, the Basel accords require banks to have a certain equity ratio to minimise the risk of bankruptcy.

In 1988, the First Basel Accord was introduced. This guideline weights on- and off-balance sheet items to estimate their risk level, which is faced by the minimum capital level. It requires an eight percent equity ratio as a minimum capital level.[8]

In 2004, Basel II and in 2010 Basel III were introduced. Basel II is based on a framework of three pillars: minimum capital requirements, supervisory review and the market discipline. Essentially, the importance of the risk involved when granting credits was heavily emphasised. Basel III extends the three pillars of Basel II and demands banks to have a 4.5 percent stake of core capital to improve liquidity in need.[9]

Basel I-III requirements have changed the banking sector, but there are significant changes for SME financing possibilities, too. A company's rating is the most important factor, when a bank decides to grant a credit. There are several qualitative, quantitative and branch specific key indicators, which influence the rating and therefore the credit's

---

[6]   Krings, Thomas, "Die Bedeutung der Lieferantenfinanzierung in der Unternehmenskrise," p. 81.
[7]   EY, "Wege zum Wachstum – Finanzierungsverhalten im deutschen Mittelstand," p. 9.
[8]   Balthazar, Laurent, *The Integration of State-of-the-Art Risk Modeling in Banking Regulation* (New York: Palgrave Macmillan, 2006), pp. 16-17.
[9]   Zirkler, Bernd, Jonathan Hofmann, and Sandra Schmolz, *Basel III in der Unternehmenspraxis* (Wiesbaden: Springer Gabler, 2015), pp. 1-4.

terms.[10] The cost of capital is highly dependent on the risk a company's rating represents for the bank. Indicators suchlike, equity ratio, cash flow, revenue and forecast influence the lending. Moreover, this increases the price for bank loans, due to rating costs or a poor rating as well as it requires SME to have a high degree of transparency towards the bank.[11] This and the dependency on the bankroller have changed the importance of company funding for SME.[12]

2.2 Importance of working capital management

The past financial crises were especially rough for SME, because they often suffered and relied on a single provider of debt capital. Therefore, upcoming investments and projects were delayed. Thus, most of the SME identified company funding and working capital management as strategic factors, which need attention on their own.[13],[14]

Current assets and liabilities represent the working capital of a company. The difference between current assets and current liabilities is defined as net working capital. Current assets are e.g. cash, marketable securities, accounts receivables and inventory. Current liabilities are e.g. short-term loans, accounts payable or accrued income taxes.[15]

Procurement, commodities management and sales are influencing the working capital, depending on the business' type and its current situation.[16]

The two main influencers of net working capital are accounts receivable and accounts payable. Accounts receivable are customers' unpaid bills, which have not been paid for right away. Companies often grant a trade or consumer credit for their customers (either business or individual customers), which is free of charge or has cash discount for prompt payment. Accounts payable are outstanding payments to other companies for received goods or services.[17]

---

[10] Hofmann, Jonathan, and Sandra Schmolz, *Controlling und Basel III in der Unternehmenspraxis: Strategien zur Bewältigung erhöhter Bonitätsanforderungen* (Wiesbaden: Springer Gabler, 2014), pp. 52-56.

[11] Fischl, Bernd, *Alternative Unternehmensfinanzierung für den deutschen Mittelstand*, 2nd ed. (Wiesbaden: Gabler Verlag, 2011), pp. 10-11.

[12] EY, "Wege zum Wachstum – Finanzierungsverhalten im deutschen Mittelstand," p. 15.

[13] Ibid.

[14] Krings, Thomas, "Die Bedeutung der Lieferantenfinanzierung in der Unternehmenskrise," p. 81.

[15] Brealey, Richard A., Myers, Stewart C., and Alan J. Marcus, *Fundamentals of Corporate Finance*, 3rd ed. (McGraw-Hill Higher Education, 2001), p. 167.

[16] Eckstein, A., Liebetrau, A., and A. Funk-Münchmeyer, *Insurance & Innovation 2017 – Ideen und Erfolgskonzepte von Experten aus der Praxis*, p. 91.

[17] Brealey, Richard A., Myers, Stewart C., and Alan J. Marcus, *Fundamentals of Corporate Finance*, pp.167-168.

The main task of working capital management is to ensure liquidity. Therefore, the right amount of cash and cash equivalents must be available to be able to pay the accounts payable. Simultaneously, the conversion of accounts receivable into cash has to be taken into account to plan the company funding.[18]

Figure 1: Cash conversion cycle[19]

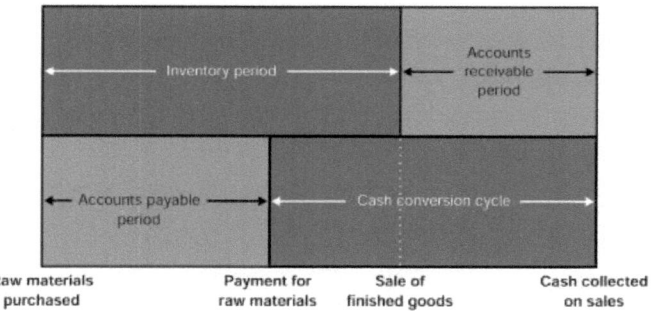

Figure 1 shows the cash conversion cycle, which is split in four different periods. First, a company purchases raw materials, which are not paid instantly. The raw materials are manufactured into products. Therefore, the accounts payable period starts at the same time as the inventory period. As soon as the finished products are sold the inventory period ends and the accounts receivable period starts. In the meantime, the payment for the raw materials is made. The cash conversion cycle starts from this point on and ends, when the customers pay for their received products.[20] To bypass the period between paying for the raw materials and receiving cash from the customer needs a planned company funding to ensure liquidity. Finetrading and factoring are methods to shorten the cash conversion cycle.

---

[18] Eckstein, A., Liebetrau, A., and A. Funk-Münchmeyer, *Insurance & Innovation 2017 – Ideen und Erfolgskonzepte von Experten aus der Praxis*, p. 91.
[19] Brealey, Richard A., Myers, Stewart C., and Alan J. Marcus, *Fundamentals of Corporate Finance*, p.169.
[20] Ibid., pp. 168-169.

3 Finetrading and factoring – methods of company funding

In 2013, an E&Y survey revealed a changing behaviour of companies choosing their financial partners and methods. The survey compares the results to a former. The most important company funding method is internal financing by cash flow or retained income. Bank loans lost in importance and alternative methods suchlike leasing, factoring, outside investors or mezzanine capital have massively increased their importance.[21] Moreover, the study has shown an increase in companies using a differentiated mix of funding methods and companies. Those companies are growing faster than firms relying on traditional financing methods.[22] Finetrading, factoring and reverse factoring are such alternative company funding methods and are examined in the next subchapters. All methods are alternatives to a traditional trade credit and accelerate the cash conversion cycle as well as they improve e.g. the cash flow.[23]

3.1 Finetrading

Finetrading is a method, which can be used to finance sales or purchases.[24] It is a commercial transaction and can be defined as a drop-shipping transaction. The Banking Act does not affect Finetraders, therefore they are not supervised by the Federal Financial Supervisory Authority.[25] The main goals are extending the date of payment, decreasing the capital lockup and receiving cash discounts for prompt payments. A trade intermediary (the finetrading association) offers a drop-shipping transaction, where the finetrader pre-finances the purchases of goods of a customer (customer of the drop-shipping). The finetrader grants an extended and flexible period of payment for which he demands a deferral and keeps the cash discount for prompt payment. Besides the deferral, an additional charge is payable, which depends on the frame agreement and the limit.[26] Figure 2 depicts the relation between supplier, buyer and finetrader.

The customer/debtor and the finetrader arrange a frame agreement, which enables the debtor to pre-finance several purchases from different suppliers up to an agreed limit.

[21] EY, "Wege zum Wachstum – Finanzierungsverhalten im deutschen Mittelstand," p. 18.
[22] Ibid., pp. 22-23.
[23] Pike, Richard, and Bill Neale, *Corporate Finance and Investment: Decisions & Strategies*, 5th ed. (Harlow: Financial Times Prentice Hall, 2006), pp. 385-387.
[24] Wöltje, Jörg, *Investition und Finanzierung*, 2nd ed. (Freiburg: Haufe Gruppe, 2017), p. 476.
[25] Koch, Sven, and Tim Schade, "Mit Finetrading den Factoring-Umsatz steigern," *FLF – Finanzierung Leasing Factoring* 3 (2015), p. 138.
[26] Koch, Sven, "Finetrading versus Reverse Factoring: Fremdfinanzierungsinstrumente zur Working Capital-Optimierung," *Corporate Finance* 11 (2014), pp. 461-462.

The suppliers are not included within the frame agreement. A credit check of the debtor is performed, which includes commercial credit insurance. The maximum insurability is the maximum finetrading limit.[27]

Figure 2: Exemplary procedure of finetrading[28]

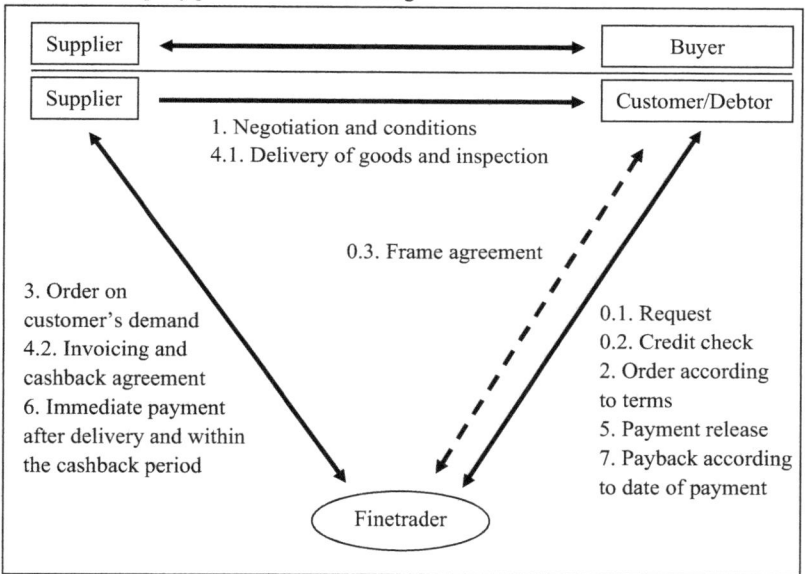

After the frame agreement between finetrader and debtor is closed, the debtor negotiates the purchase of goods with the supplier. Subsequently, the debtor orders the goods at the finetrader. The finetrader contracts a purchase agreement with the supplier on basis of the previous negotiations between supplier and buyer and additionally with the debtor. The finetrader orders the delivery of goods and the supplier delivers them directly to the customer/debtor. Therefore, the finetrader is creditor towards the supplier and del credere agent towards the debtor. When the debtor has inspected and confirmed the goods, the finetrader pays the supplier's invoice within the cashback period. As long as the debtor has not fully paid the goods and charges to the finetrader, the finetrader is the owner of the goods. According to the agreement between debtor and finetrader, the

[27] Koch, Sven, "Finetrading versus Reverse Factoring: Fremdfinanzierungsinstrumente zur Working Capital-Optimierung," pp. 461-462.
[28] According to: Koch, Sven, "Finetrading versus Reverse Factoring: Fremdfinanzierungsinstrumente zur Working Capital-Optimierung," p. 462.

debtor has several months to pay for the goods flexibly.[29] The procedure shown in figure 2 represents a merchandise financing. Other forms are market financing and warehouse financing. Market financing is identical to merchandise financing procedure, but the supplier uses finetrading to acquire new customers or markets. Warehouse financing needs an additional consignment stock, which has certain goods available for the buyer.

3.2 Factoring

In 2016, the turnover of factoring increased by 3.77 percent to 216.8 billion Euro compared to 2015 (in Germany). More than 27,250 firms use factoring as a financing method.[30]

Large enterprises often have an own credit management, which collects the accounts receivable, because they experience economies of scale.[31] SME are not always able to hire such an expert but can participate in the advantages, if the accounts receivable are sold to a factor. Factoring is a financial transaction and is affected by the Banking Act.[32]

Figure 3: Market financing procedure of factoring[33]

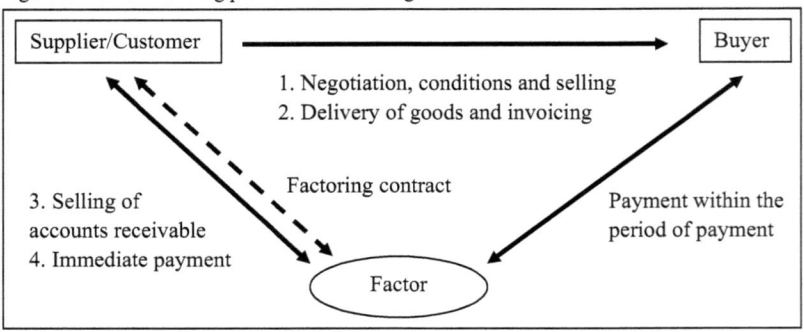

If a company decides to sell their accounts receivable to a factor, both parties agree on a factoring contract. This contract arranges the customers, which are included and their credit limits and the collection period. Factoring starts after the supplier and buyer have

[29] Koch, Sven, "Finetrading versus Reverse Factoring: Fremdfinanzierungsinstrumente zur Working Capital-Optimierung," p. 462.
[30] Deutscher Factoring Verband e.V., „The German factoring market 2016," http://www.factoring.de/german-factoring-market-2016-0, accessed August 2017.
[31] Brealey, Richard A., Myers, Stewart C., and Franklin Allen, *Principles of Corporate Finance*, 10th ed. (Boston, MA: McGraw-Hill/Irwin, 2011), p. 765.
[32] Koch, Sven, "Finetrading versus Reverse Factoring: Fremdfinanzierungsinstrumente zur Working Capital-Optimierung," p. 463.
[33] Accoring to Koch, Sven, and Tim Schade, "Mit Finetrading den Factoring-Umsatz steigern," p. 138.

negotiated the conditions of the purchase, the goods are delivered and the invoice is sent. The supplier informs his customers about the invoices sold to the factor. The supplier sends invoices to both, buyer and factor. The customers are directly paying the factor within the period of payment agreed on with the supplier. The supplier receives the payment of the invoices by the factor, whether the buyer has already paid the invoice or not. For this service, a fee is charged which usually amounts to one to two percent of the invoice's value. Moreover, the factor is able to advance a stake of about 80 percent of the accounts receivable against an additional charge.[34] Furthermore, it is possible to let the factor manage the debtors and the dunning as well as take the del credere risk.[35] Factoring which includes all services is called full-service factoring.[36]

3.3   Reverse factoring

There is an analogy between reverse factoring and finetrading. Both methods are merchandise financing methods but there are legal and financial differences.[37] As a financial transaction, it stays supervision as well as factoring. There are more contracts, extensive credit checks of all involved parties and it is timely and complex to implement. The factor buys the debts and the finetrader buys the goods. Moreover, the buyer/debtor initialises reverse factoring. The debtor and the reverse factor are closing a frame agreement and reverse factor pays the debtor's liabilities at different suppliers. The debtor pays the liabilities within a fixed but more flexible timeframe. The reverse factor contracts the suppliers mentioned in the frame agreement. Each supplier signs a factoring contract with the reverse factor. The suppliers sell their invoices to the reverse factor, who agrees to pay within the cashback payment period.[38]

---

[34]   Brealey, Richard A., Myers, Stewart C., and Franklin Allen, *Principles of Corporate Finance*, p. 765.

[35]   Fischl, Bernd, *Alternative Unternehmensfinanzierung für den deutschen Mittelstand*, p. 21.

[36]   Koch, Sven, "Finetrading versus Reverse Factoring: Fremdfinanzierungsinstrumente zur Working Capital-Optimierung," p. 463.

[37]   Eckstein, A., Liebetrau, A., and A. Funk-Münchmeyer, *Insurance & Innovation 2017 – Ideen und Erfolgskonzepte von Experten aus der Praxis*, p. 99.

[38]   Koch, Sven, "Finetrading versus Reverse Factoring: Fremdfinanzierungsinstrumente zur Working Capital-Optimierung," p. 464.

4 Finetrading and factoring – pros, cons and consequences

The further investigation is limited to finetrading and factoring. Reverse factoring is excluded due to its uncommon use in Germany. Factoring is a well-established financing method in the SME sector compared to finetrading, which is rather unknown. Factoring is a financial transaction, finetrading is not, therefore it is not under supervision and could cause some distrust in the method.[39]

4.1 Pros and cons of finetrading and factoring

Finetrading has several pros and cons for the supplier and buyer. The finetrader always pays within the cashback period. Therefore, the supplier receives the cash less discount by default, which is the only disadvantage for the supplier. Apart from this, the supplier experiences an improved planning process of liquidity and working capital due to reliable payments within the discounting period, additionally the del credere risk is gone. Finetrading causes a balance sheet contraction and improves the supplier's equity ratio. The financial reliability of the supplier increases, which is beneficial for the rating and eases the raising of credits.[40]

The customer of the finetrader has to face high volatile financing costs after the first month, which usually is free of charge due to the cashback the finetrader receives paying the supplier's invoice.[41] The finetrader grants a roll-over credit with matching maturities, which increase the solvency scope of the buyer. The bank line is relieved and the buyer has the freedom to use the gained capital for further credits instead of saving it for securities. Moreover, an increased flexibility is reached due to a free choice of suppliers. Finetrading is usually implemented within 10 days, which offers a fast improvement of e.g. the cash conversion cycle. The extended payment period offers the opportunity to increase the selling capacity. The long-term relation improves purchasing conditions and boosts the bargaining position of the buyer.[42]

Full-service factoring shortens the waiting time for the buyer's payment, which improves liquidity and the financial standing and therefore the terms of bank loans. The

---

[39] Koch, Sven, and Tim Schade, "Mit Finetrading den Factoring-Umsatz steigern," p. 138.
[40] Koch, Sven, "Finetrading versus Reverse Factoring: Fremdfinanzierungsinstrumente zur Working Capital-Optimierung," p. 469.
[41] Koch, Sven, "Finetrader – Konkurrent oder Partner der Hausbank?," *Kreditwesen* 5 (2015), p. 248.
[42] Koch, Sven, "Finetrading versus Reverse Factoring: Fremdfinanzierungsinstrumente zur Working Capital-Optimierung," p. 469.

accounts receivable are decreased and the supplier is able to pay invoices from other suppliers much faster. This faster payment within the cashback period creates a disposition advantage. The factor bears the del credere and the payment default risks. Again, a balance sheet contraction and optimisation of working capital is reached. Moreover, the factor's customer is able to focus on his core business, the debtor management and the dunning is relieved or completely outsourced. [43]

Otherwise, the contact with customers is decreased and a strict or rough dunning could damage the customer's relationship. Factoring agreements often last several years and the reintegration of outsourced departments is challenging. Additionally, customers might be reluctant towards factoring or the factor and the company introducing factoring might face a loss of image.[44]

4.2   Consequences for the working capital and the balance sheet

Factoring and finetrading help to manage working capital. There is always a trade-off between the current assets' carrying and shortage costs. It is the financial manager's responsibility to balance the current assets' costs and benefits.[45]

Both methods are able to shorten the cash conversion cycle. As depicted in figure 1, on the one hand, the accounts payable period can be extended using finetrading. On the other hand, factoring is useful to shorten the accounts receivable period. The implementation of either factoring or finetrading is shortening the cash conversion cycle, leading to an increased liquidity. Implementing both methods as a company decreases the cash conversion cycle to a minimum.[46] This is helpful for companies having a very long production process or long-term projects (long inventory period), which are sold to customers located in regions with poor payment morale. Therefore, both instruments are not competing but complementary.

In a finetrading procedure, the supplier's current assets in the balance sheet are altered. The finetrader pays the supplier's accounts receivable, therefore the suppliers receives cash. If this is used to pay accounts payable, the balance sheet is contracted. The debtor

[43]   Wöltje, Jörg, *Investition und Finanzierung*, pp. 465-475.
[44]   Ibid.
[45]   Brealey, Richard A., Myers, Stewart C., and Alan J. Marcus, *Fundamentals of Corporate Finance*, p. 171.
[46]   Koch, Sven, and Tim Schade, "Mit Finetrading den Factoring-Umsatz steigern," pp. 138-139.

has an extended period to pay the accounts payable to the finetrader, therefore cash can be accumulated or invested in inventory.

In a factoring procedure, the supplier sells the accounts receivable to the factor. In exchange, he receives most of the invoice as cash immediately. Again, the supplier can use this cash to pay his accounts payable to other suppliers to contract the balance.

5   Conclusion

Concluding, factoring and finetrading are competitive and innovative company funding methods. They are enablers for working capital optimisation and extraordinary suitable for shortening the cash conversion cycle. Especially, SME are able to benefit from these methods. Moreover, the access is easier for them and the implementation is fast particularly for finetrading.

Both methods are well-positioned alternatives to a traditional bank loan or trade credit. The past growth rates are promising for both methods, especially factoring booms in times of difficult credit check procedures. Companies with a high level of solvency can use both methods for further optimisation and large companies are able to provide their customers both as an in-house service, increasing the customer loyalty.

Factoring is already well-established but finetrading is commonly unfamiliar. The extended payment period can influence the buying decision. German SME exporting goods globally can highly capitalize on this advantage.

Overall, both methods will increase in their importance, as long as current financial situation in Germany remains status quo.

Bibliography

Balthazar, Laurent. *The Integration of State-of-the-Art Risk Modeling in Banking Regulation*. New York: Palgrave Macmillan, 2006.

Brealey, Richard A., Myers, Stewart C., and Alan J. Marcus. *Fundamentals of Corporate Finance*. 3rd ed. McGraw-Hill Higher Education, 2001.

Brealey, Richard A., Myers, Stewart C., and Franklin Allen. *Principles of Corporate Finance*, 10th ed. Boston: McGraw-Hill/Irwin, 2011.

Eckstein, A., Liebetrau, A., and A. Funk-Münchmeyer. *Insurance & Innovation 2017 – Ideen und Erfolgskonzepte von Experten aus der Praxis*. Karlsruhe: Verlag Versicherungswirtschaft GmbH, 2017.

Fischl, Bernd. *Alternative Unternehmensfinanzierung für den deutschen Mittelstand*. 2nd ed. Wiesbaden: Gabler Verlag, 2011.

Hofmann, Jonathan, and Sandra Schmolz. *Controlling und Basel III in der Unternehmenspraxis: Strategien zur Bewältigung erhöhter Bonitätsanforderungen*. Wiesbaden: Springer Gabler, 2014.

Koch, Sven. "Finetrader – Konkurrent oder Partner der Hausbank?." *Kreditwesen* 5 (2015), pp. 248-251.

Koch, Sven. "Finetrading versus Reverse Factoring: Fremdfinanzierungsinstrumente zur Working Capital-Optimierung." *Corporate Finance* 11 (2014), pp. 460-469.

Koch, Sven, and Tim Schade. "Mit Finetrading den Factoring-Umsatz steigern." *FLF – Finanzierung Leasing Factoring* 3 (2015), pp. 136-140.

Krings, Thomas. "Die Bedeutung der Lieferantenfinanzierung in der Unternehmenskrise." In *Refinanzieren statt Sanieren? – Unternehmen und Statten in der Krise*, edited by Werner F. Ebke, Christopher Seagon, Michael Blatz. Baden-Baden: Nomos Verlagsgesellschaft, 2014.

Pike, Richard, and Bill Neale. *Corporate Finance and Investment: Decisions & Strategies*. 5th ed. Harlow: Financial Times Prentice Hall, 2006.

Wöltje, Jörg. *Investition und Finanzierung*. 2nd ed. Freiburg: Haufe Gruppe, 2017.

Zirkler, Bernd, Jonathan Hofmann, and Sandra Schmolz. *Basel III in der Unternehmenspraxis* .Wiesbaden: Springer Gabler, 2015.

Internet bibliography

Deutscher Factoring Verband e.V. „The German factoring market 2016."
http://www.factoring.de/german-factoring-market-2016-0, accessed August 2017.

Statistisches Bundesamt. "Insolvenzen."
https://www.destatis.de/DE/ZahlenFakten/Indikatoren/LangeReihen/Insolvenzen/l
rins01.html;jsessionid=94B634D2EF272178D6D8092018C2007B.cae2, accessed
August 2017.

Statistisches Bundesamt. "Anteile kleiner und mittlerer Unternehmen an ausgewählten
Merkmalen 2014."
https://www.destatis.de/DE/ZahlenFakten/GesamtwirtschaftUmwelt/Unternehmen
Handwerk/KleineMittlereUnternehmenMittelstand/Tabellen/Insgesamt.html, accessed August 2017.